NOTE-FOR-NOTE
KEYBOARD
TRANSCRIPTIONS

KEYBOARD
Instrumentals

T0078992

ISBN 978-1-4768-7166-0

HAL•LEONARD®
CORPORATION

7777 W. BLUEMOUND RD. P.O. BOX 13819 MILWAUKEE, WI 53213

Visit Hal Leonard Online at
www.halleonard.com

Alley Cat

By Frank Bjorn

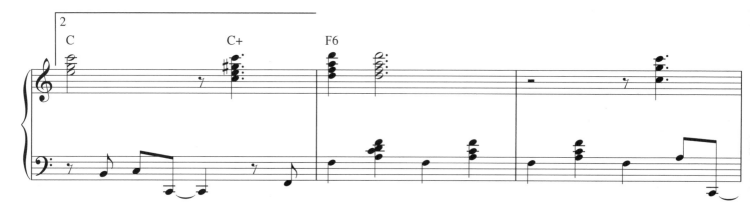

Asia Minor

By James Wisner

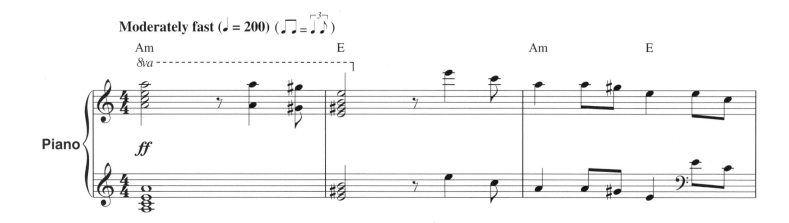

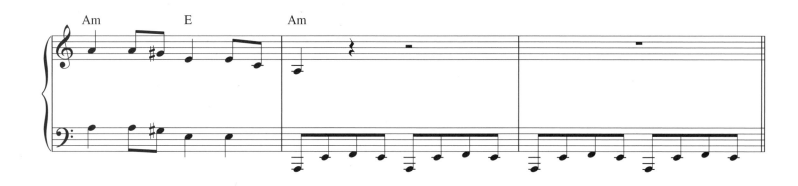

Beatnik Fly

Words and Music by Ira Mack and Tom King

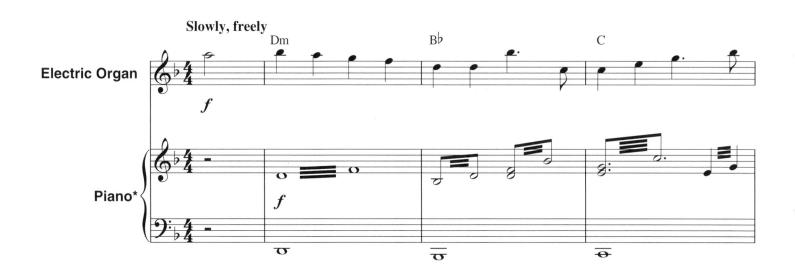

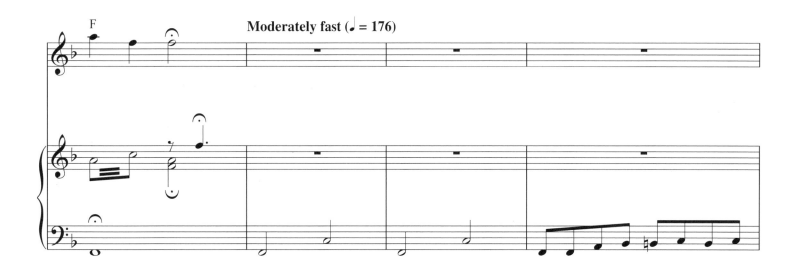

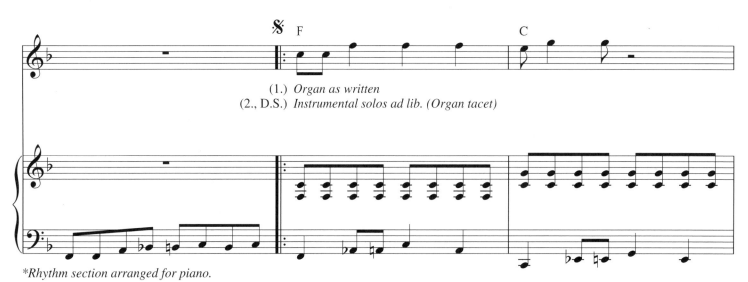

(1.) *Organ as written*
(2., D.S.) *Instrumental solos ad lib. (Organ tacet)*

Rhythm section arranged for piano.

Celestial Soda Pop

Composed by Ray Lynch

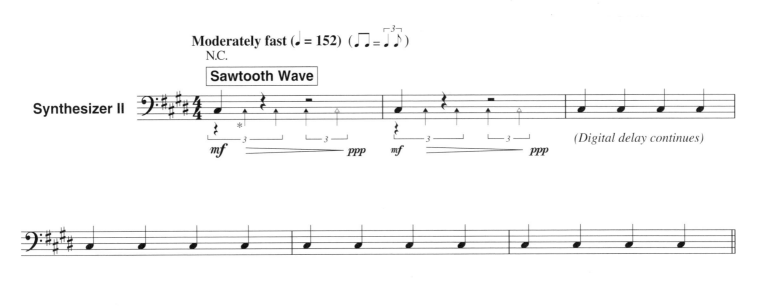

*Triangular noteheads represent digital delay as recorded on Synthesizer II.

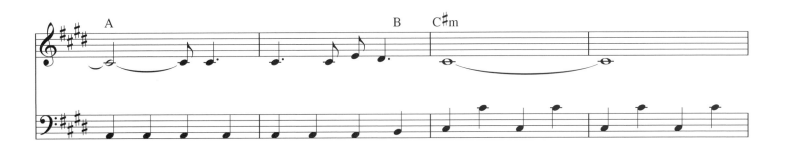

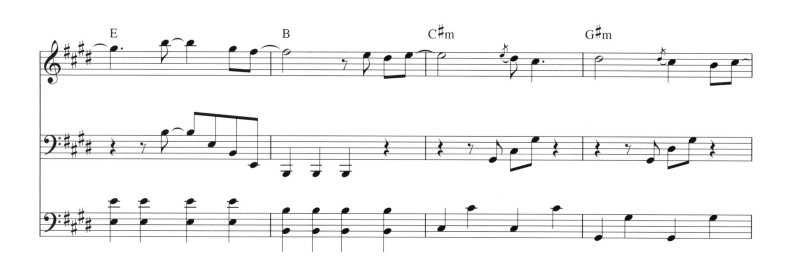

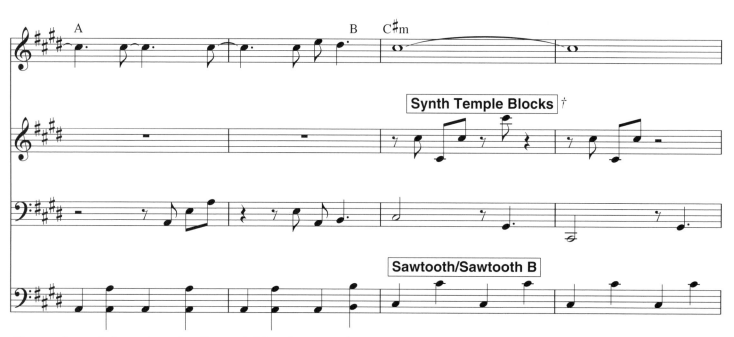

†*Two synth sounds layered together. Sawtooth B has slower attack.*

Synth Harp II

8va

(8va)

**Triangular noteheads represent digital delay as recorded on Synthesizer II.

(Gradually fade Sawtooth B from layered synth)

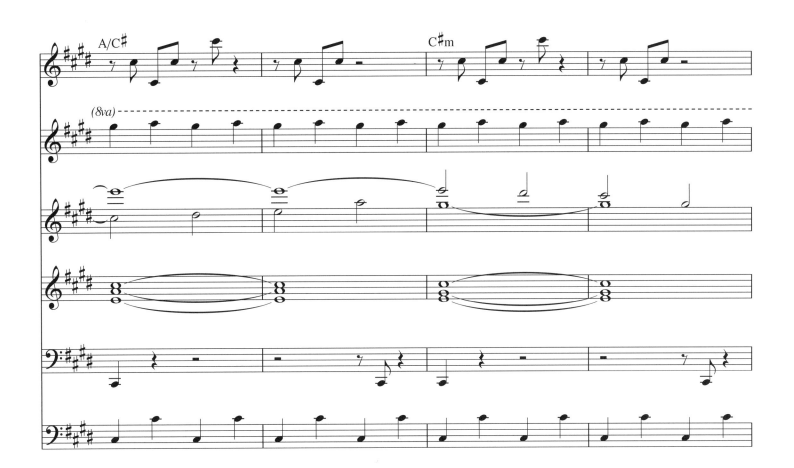

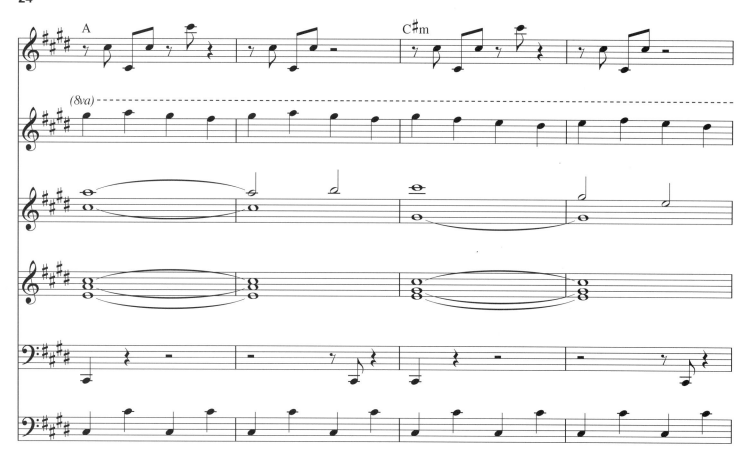

Sawtooth/Sawtooth B

Synth Harp II

(Digital delay continues to end)

8va to end-------------------->

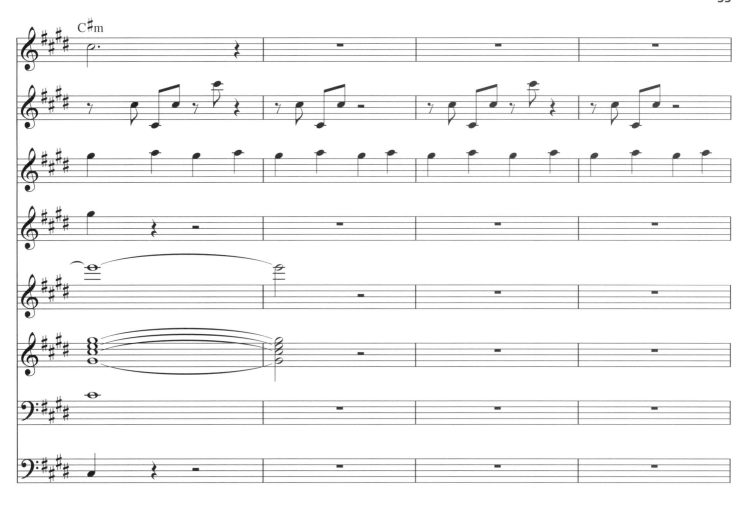

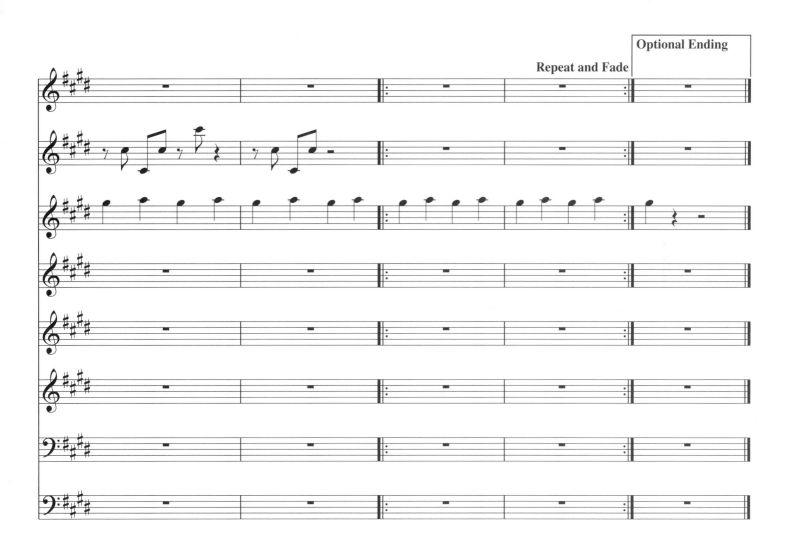

Daybreaker

By Jeff Lynne

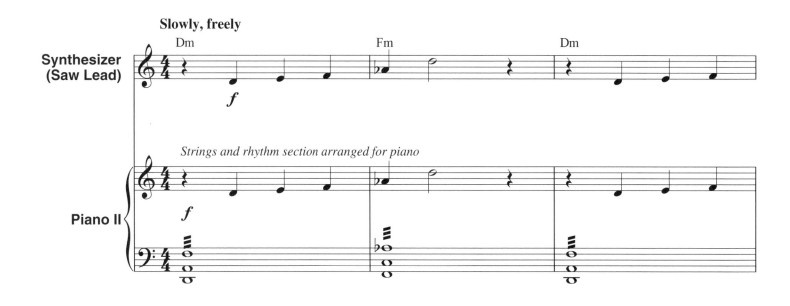

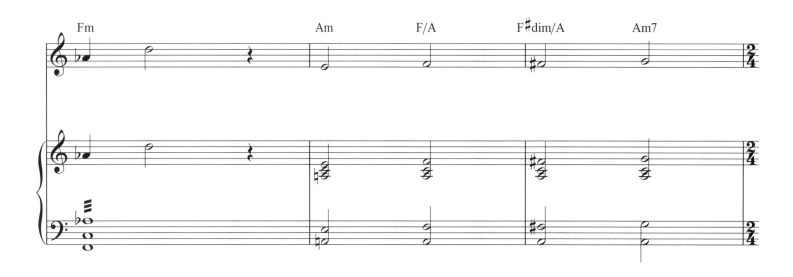

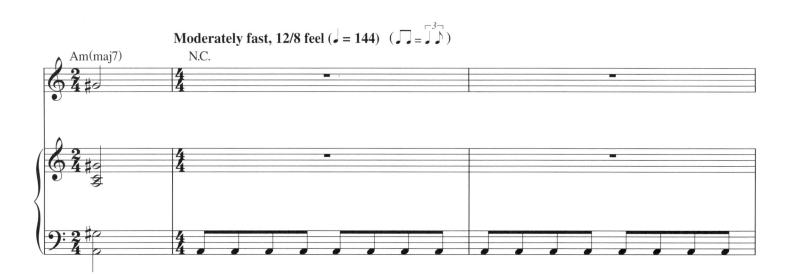

*Piano I: Piano as recorded.

Green Onions

Written by Al Jackson, Jr., Lewis Steinberg,
Booker T. Jones and Steve Cropper

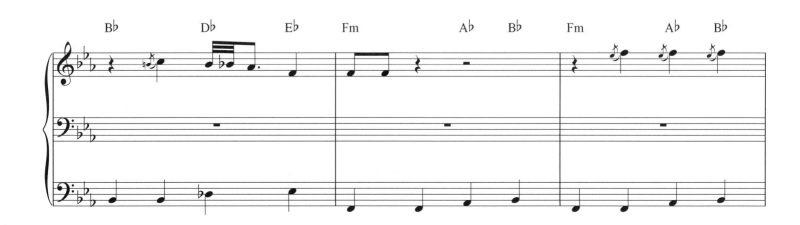

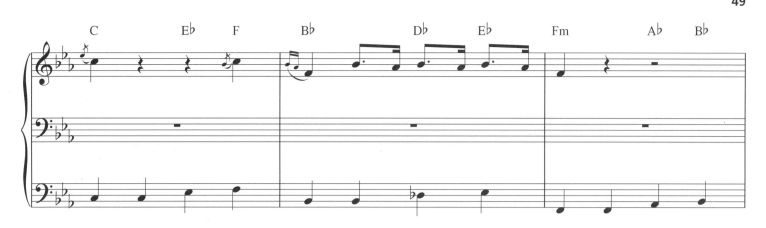

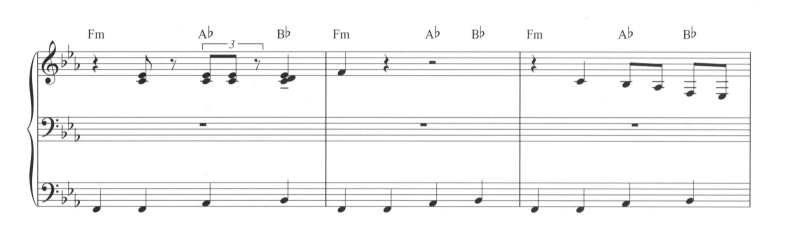

Guitar arranged for keyboard.

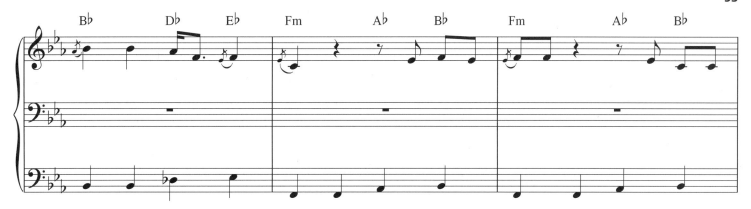

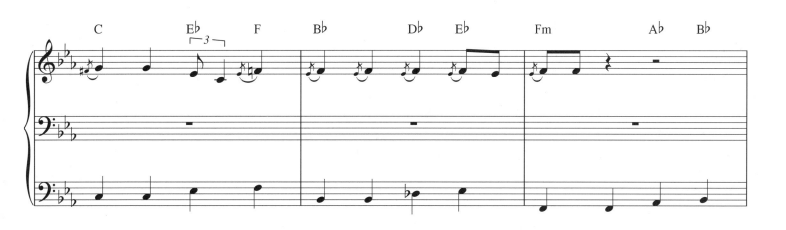

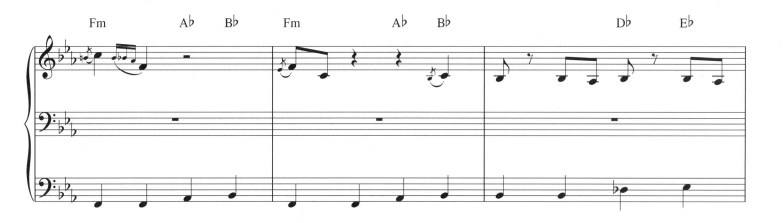

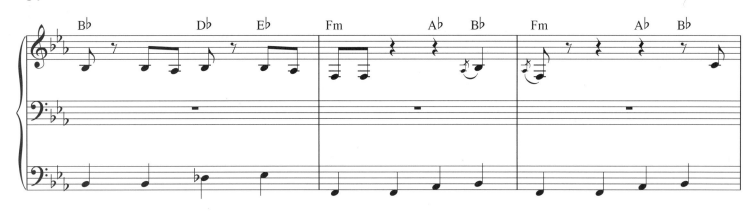

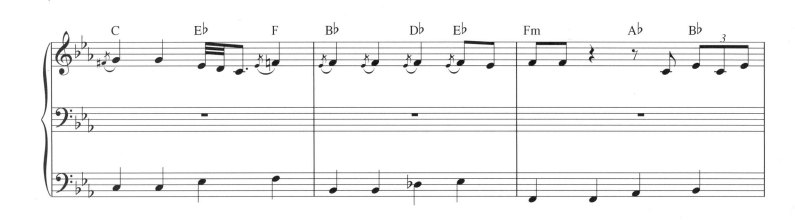

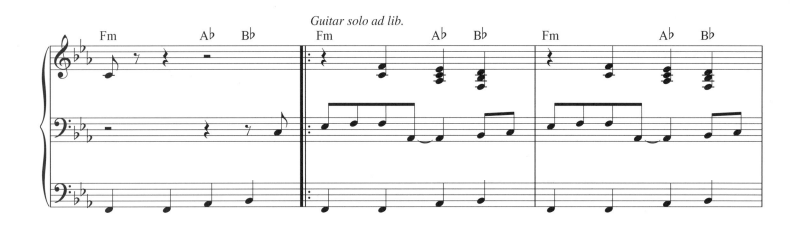

Guitar solo ad lib.

Repeat and Fade | **Optional Ending**

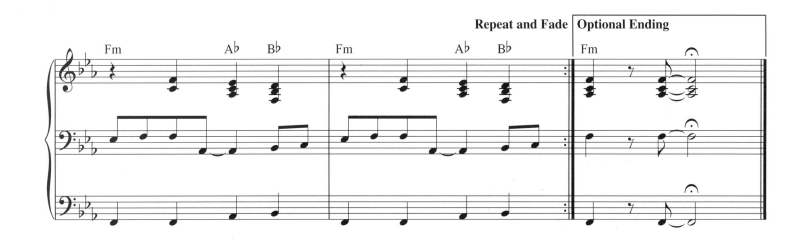

Hang 'em High

By Dominic Frontiere

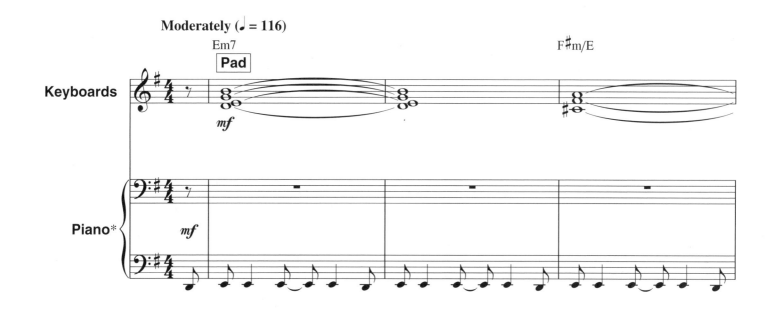

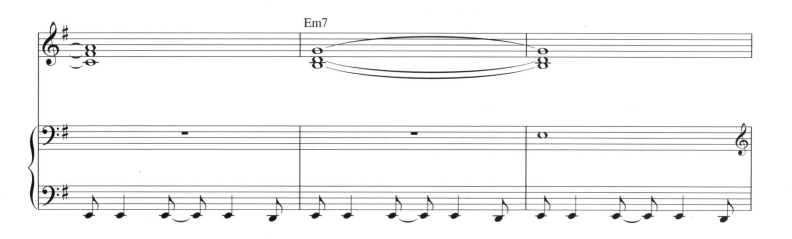

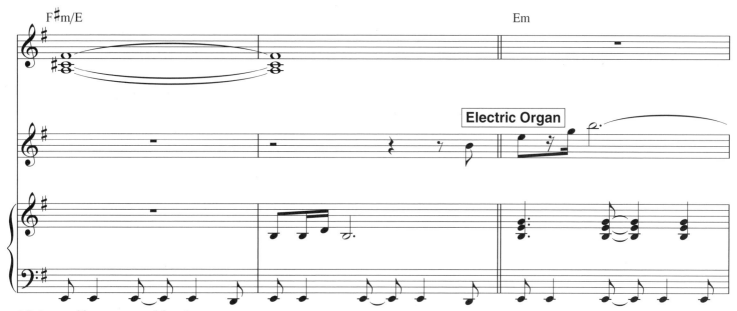

*Guitar and bass arranged for piano.

The Happy Organ

By Ken Wood, David Clowney and James Kriegsmann

*Bass arranged for piano L.H.
†(Piano L.H. as recorded)

(Guitar solo ad lib. to end)

The "In" Crowd

Words and Music by Billy Page

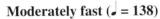

*Bass arranged for keyboard.

(Bass: optional ad lib. to end)

Joy

By J.S. Bach
Arranged by Tom Parker

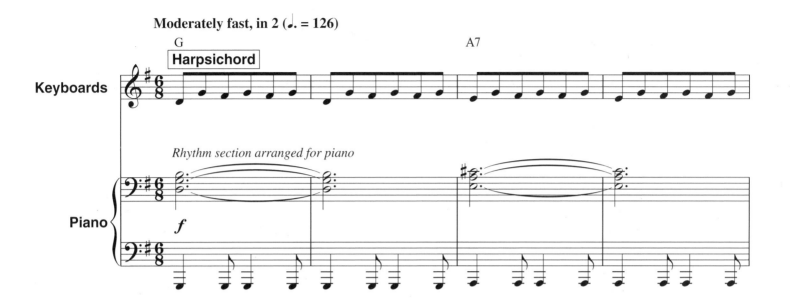

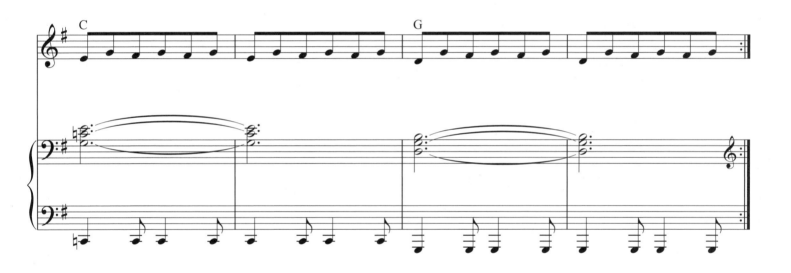

Last Date

By Floyd Cramer

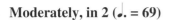

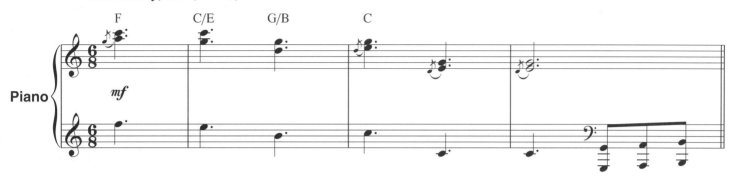

(String melody ends)

D.S. al Coda

Final chord: Piano plays R.H. only. The chord written in bass clef is played by guitar and strings.

Last Night

Words and Music by Charles Axton, Gilbert Caple, Chips Moman, Floyd Newman and Jerry Smith

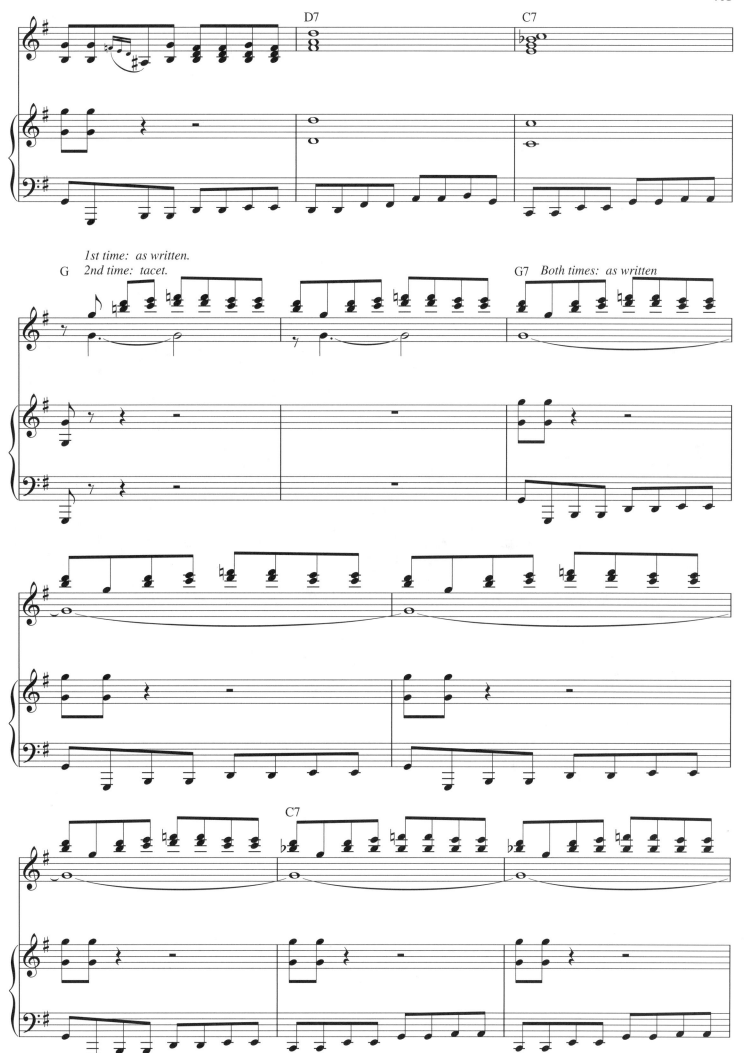

(Spoken): Oh, _____ last night.

Oh, _____ last night.

Sax solo ad lib.

Piano as recorded (both hands)

Look-Ka-Py Py

Words and Music by Leo Nocentelli, George Porter, Arthur Neville and Joseph Modeliste

(Organ tacet to end)

Drum fill- -

Play 4 times

G7

(Ook - a - chee uh.)   (Ook - a - chee ah.)   Boun - chy - boun - boun. ___ (Ook - a - chee - uh.)   (Ook - a - chee - ah.)

(Guitar arranged for piano)

Boun - chy-boun - boun. _____
(Ook - a - chee - uh.)
(Ook-a - chee - ah.)
Boun - chy-boun - boun. _
(Ook - a - chee - uh.)

_____ (Ook-a - chee - ah.)
Boun - chy-boun - boun. _____
(Ook - a - chee - uh.)
(Ook-a - chee - ah.)

Boun - chy-boun - boun. _____
(Ook - a - chee - uh.)
Boun - chy-boun - boun. _
(Ook a - chee - ah.)
(Ook - a - chee - uh.)

(Ook - a - chee - ah.)
Boun - chy-boun - boun. _____
(Ook - a - chee - ah.)
(Ook - a - chee - uh.)

Machine Gun

Words and Music by Milan Williams

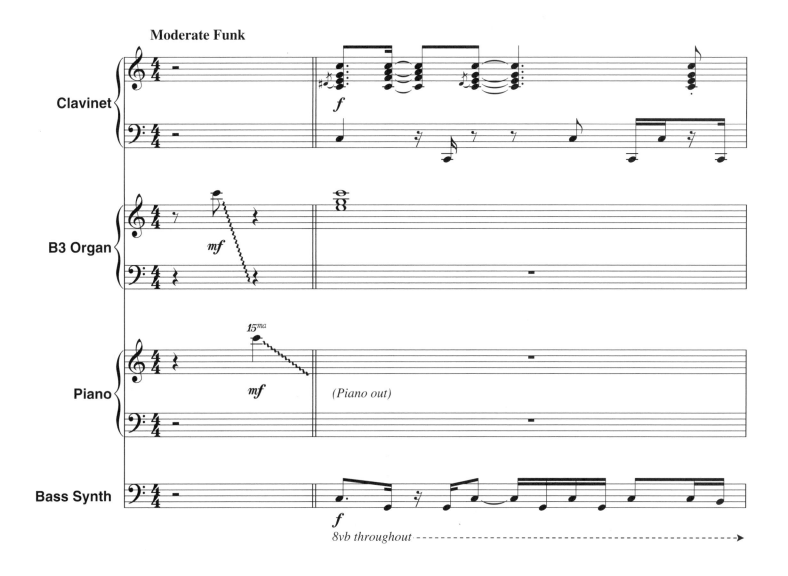

(Synth 1 out)

(Piano out)

Synth 1

(Synth 1 out)

Synth 1 *(pan: alternate R-L)*

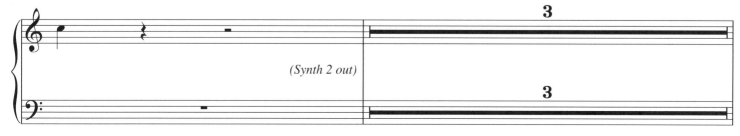

Synth 1

dim. poco a poco

mp

(Synth 1 out)

Synth 2:

Repeat and Fade

Miami Vice
Theme from the Universal Television Series
By Jan Hammer

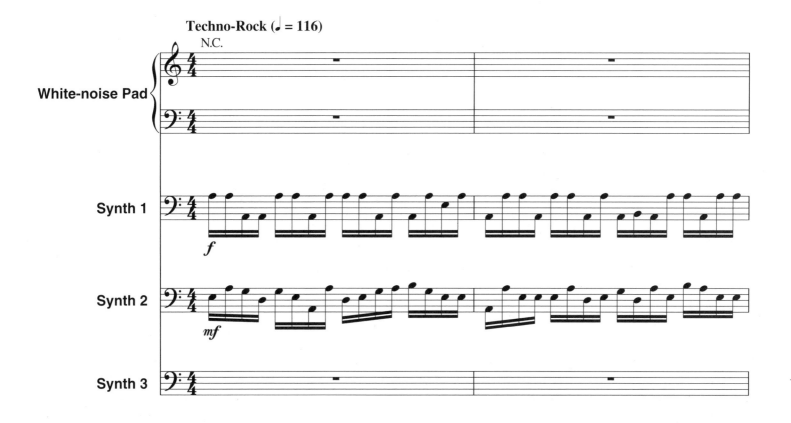

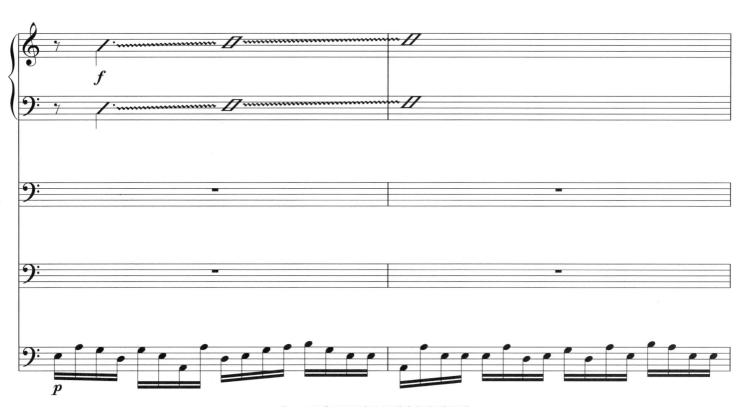

Pad

f

mp

White noise synth out

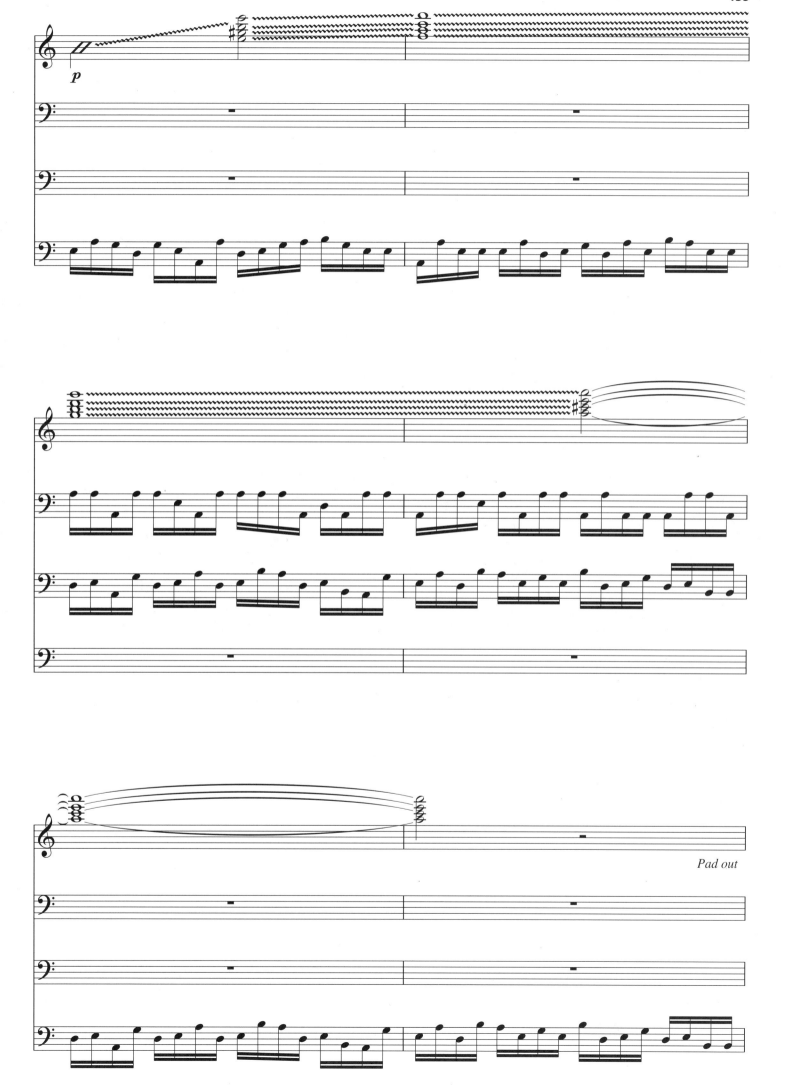

Pad out

Synth 3 out

Rhythm Guitar 2 out

Sitar synth out

G5

Gamelan synth out

Guitar 1 out

Synth 1 out

Synth 2 out

N.C.

f

Foghorn synth

ff

Outa-Space

Words and Music by Billy Preston and Joseph Greene

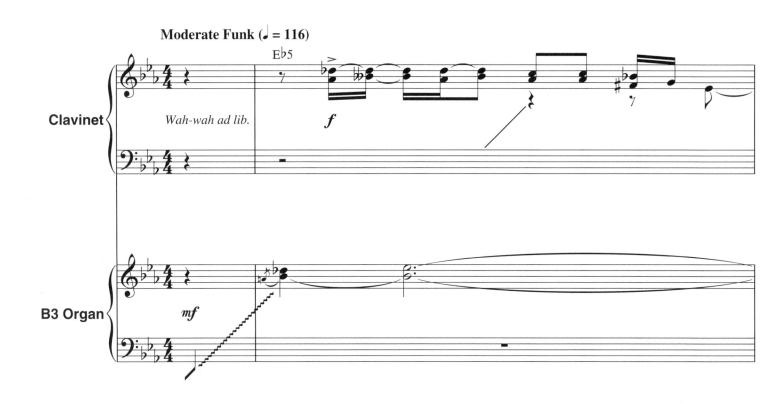

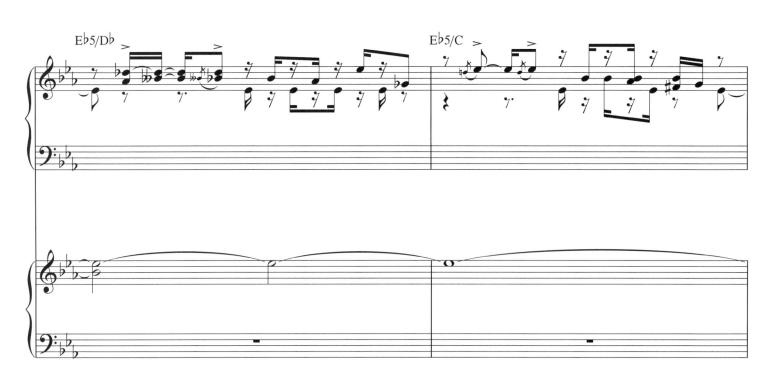

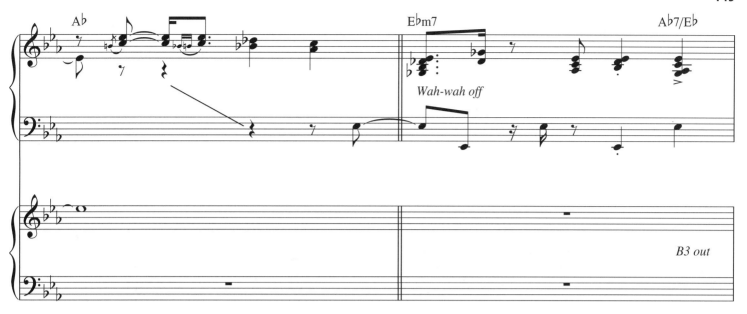

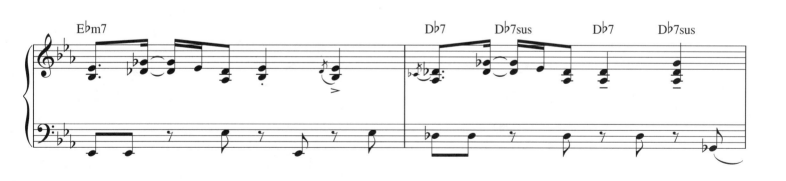

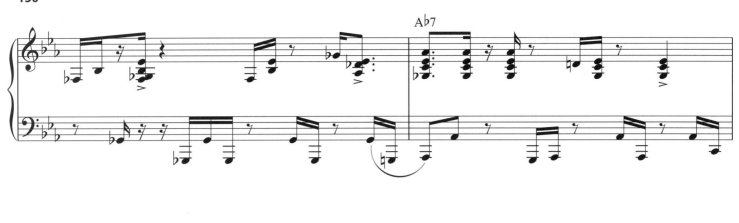

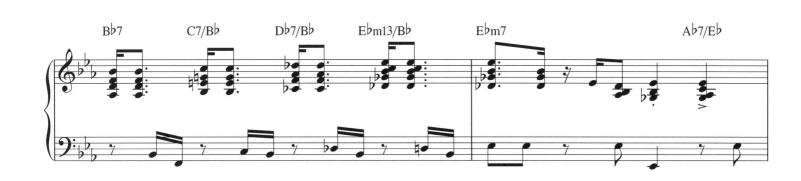

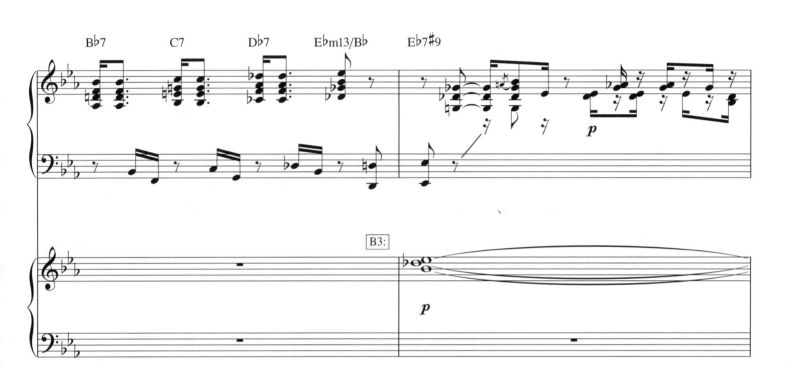

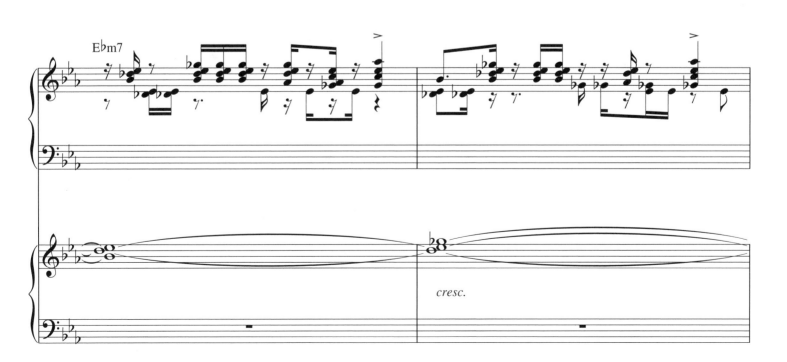

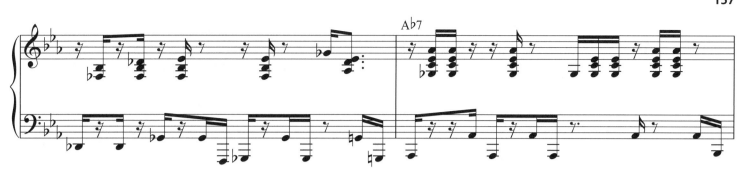

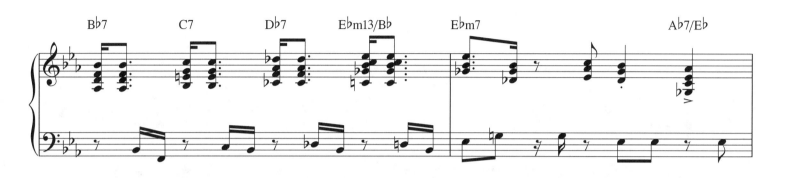

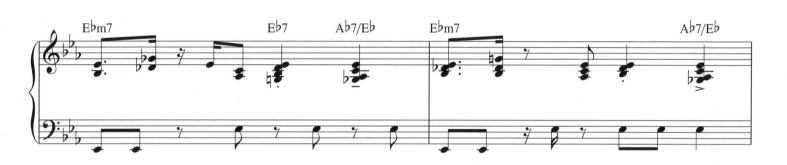

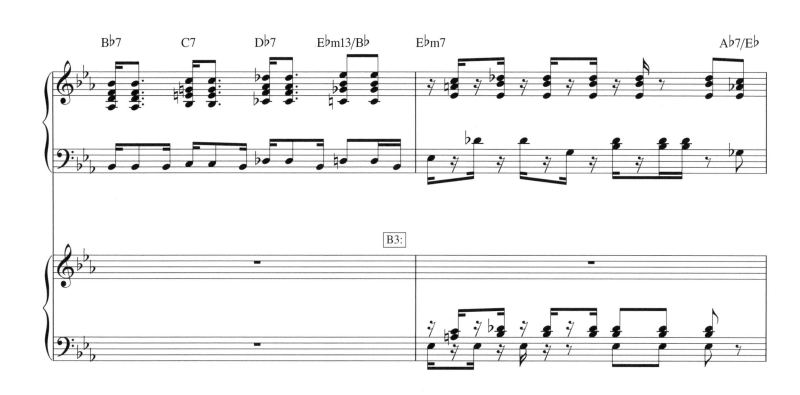

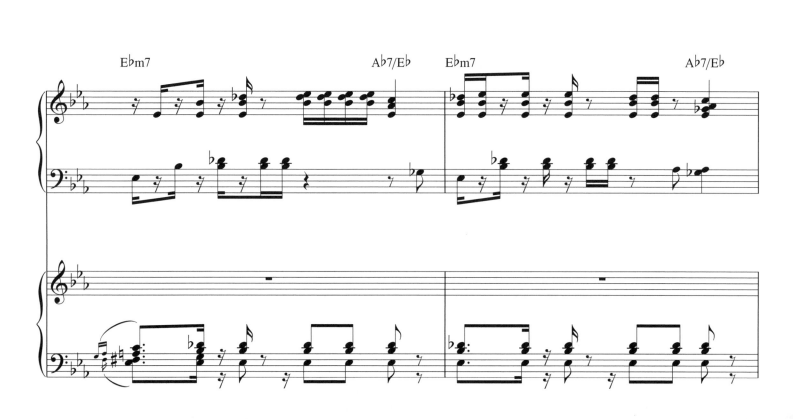

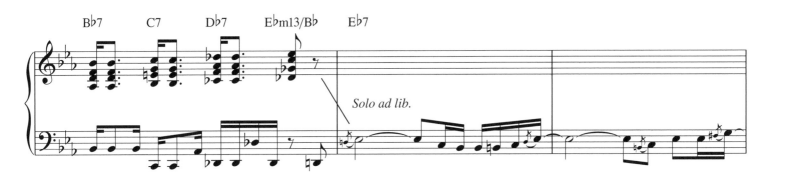

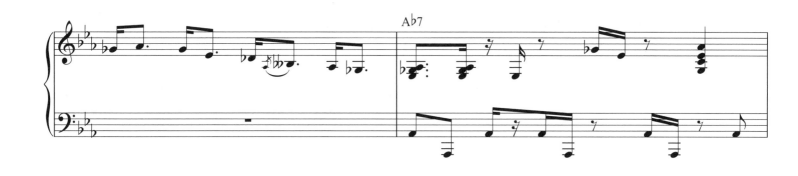

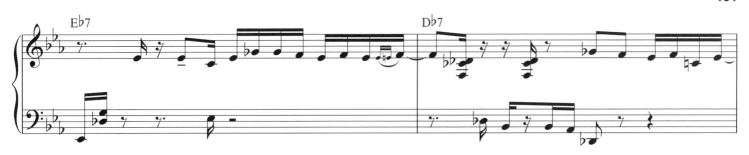

Popcorn

Music by Gershon Kingsley

Moderately fast (♩ = 132)

Lead Synth 1

Synth 1

Synth Bass

Bass Guitar (cues)

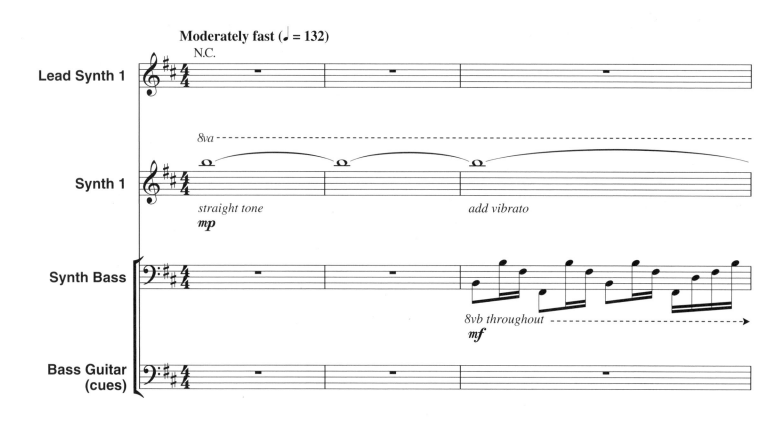

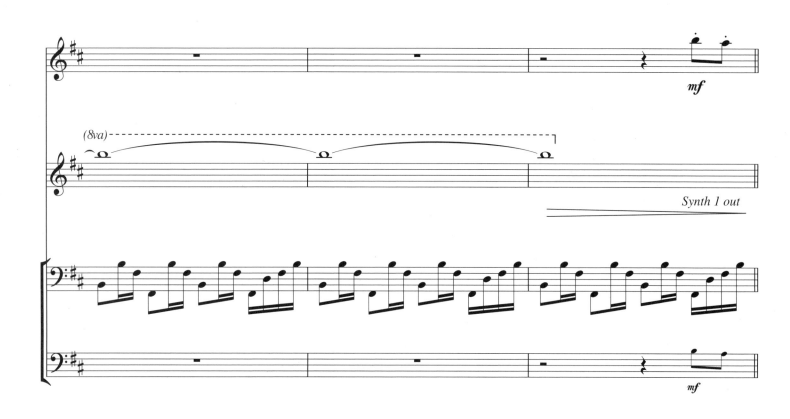

Electric bass continues sim.

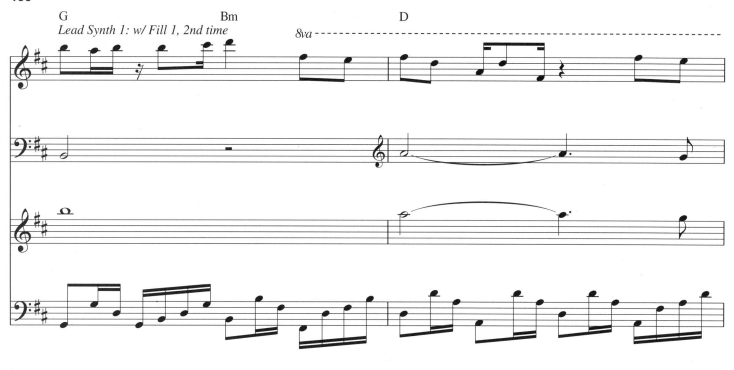

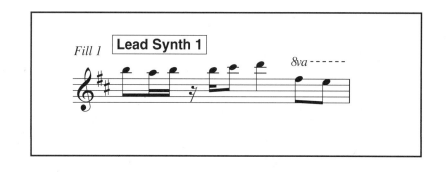

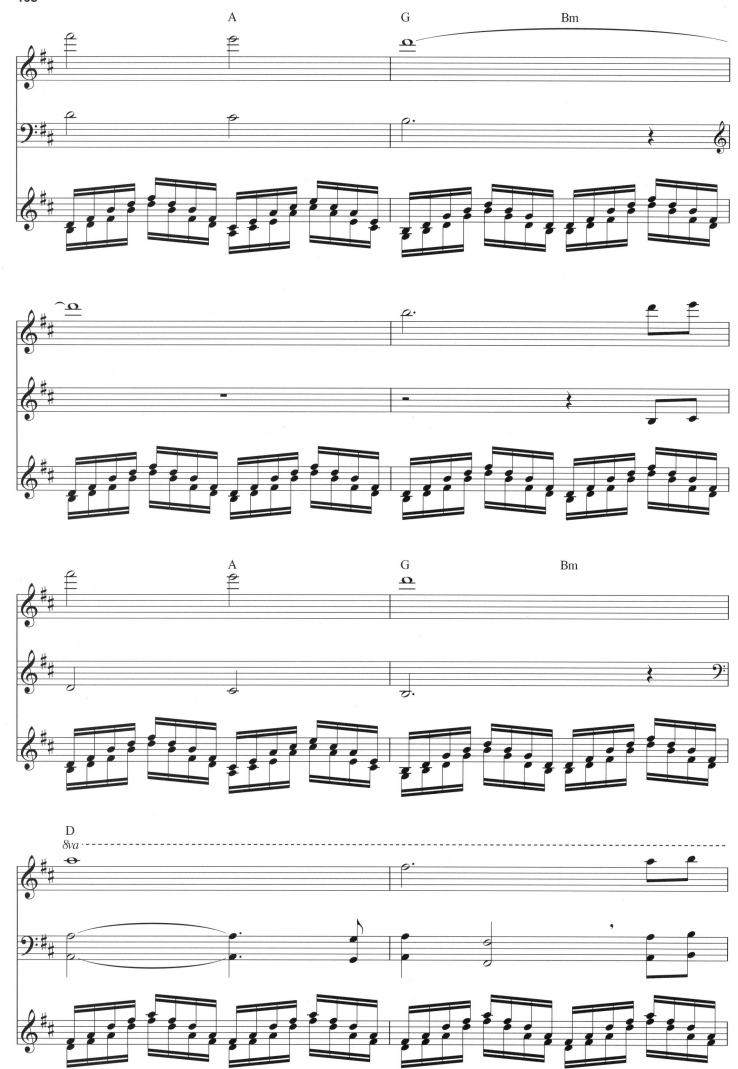

Red River Rock

By Tom King, Ira Mack and Fred Mendelsohn

Rock and Roll (straight 8ths) (♩ = 152)

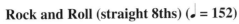

Rock Organ

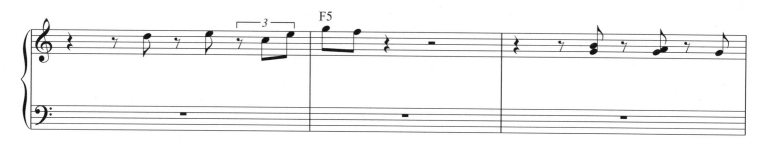

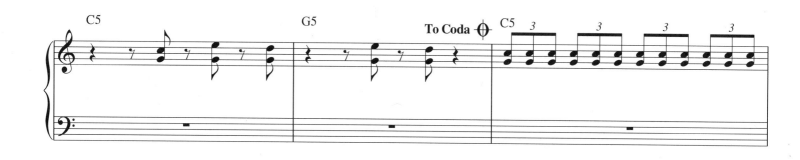

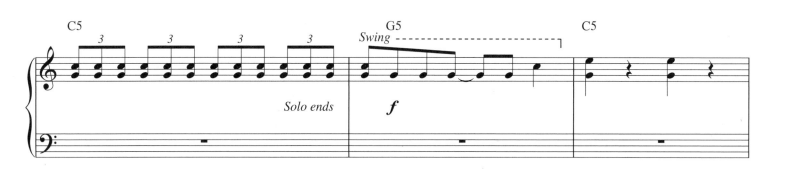

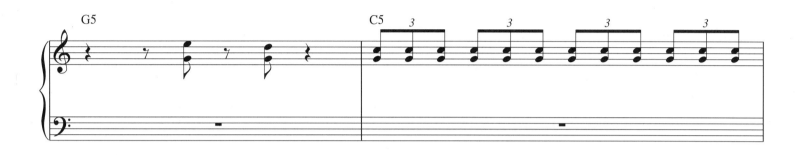

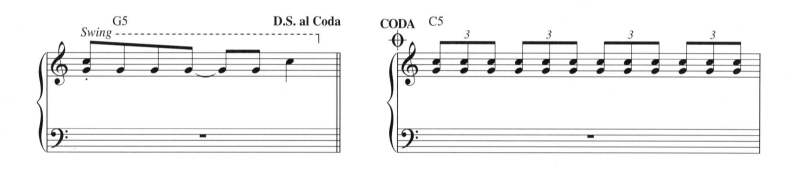

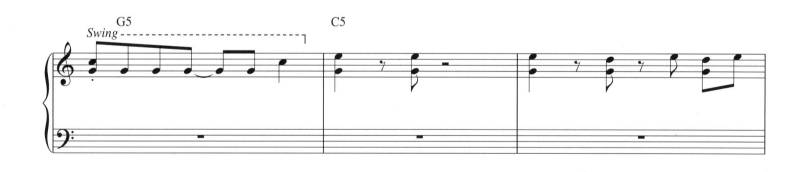

Time Is Tight

Words and Music by Booker T. Jones, Duck Dunn, Steve Cropper and Al Jackson, Jr.

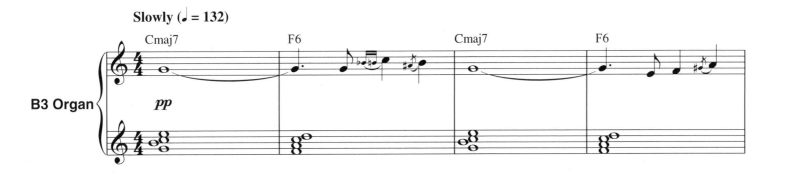

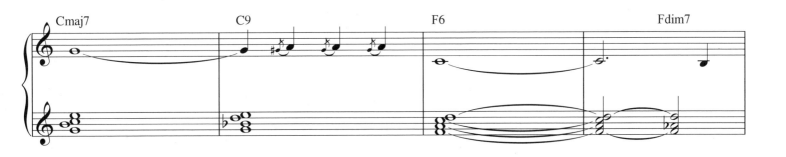

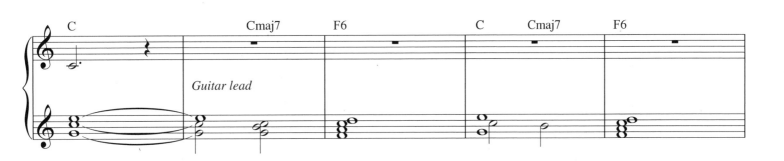

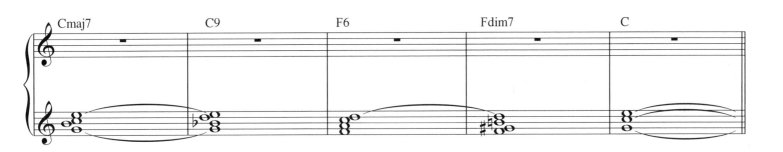

Fast Rock

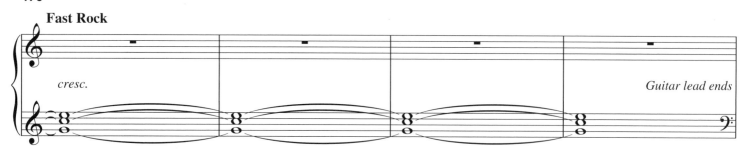

cresc.

Guitar lead ends

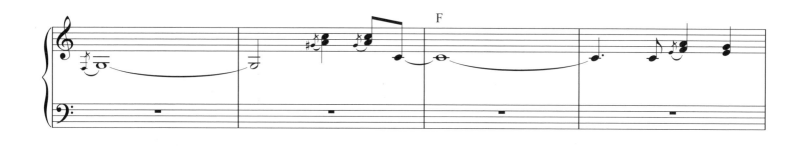

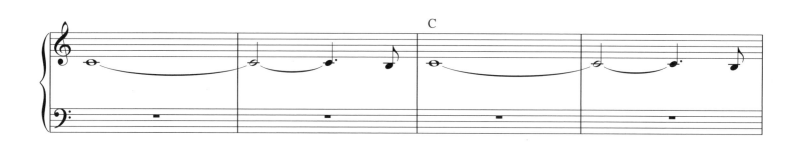

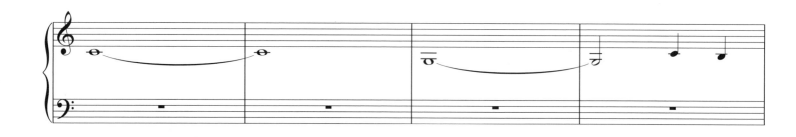

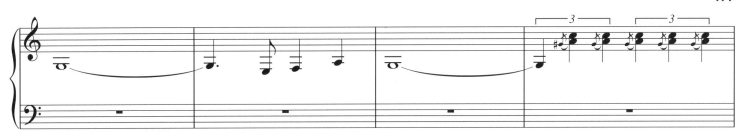

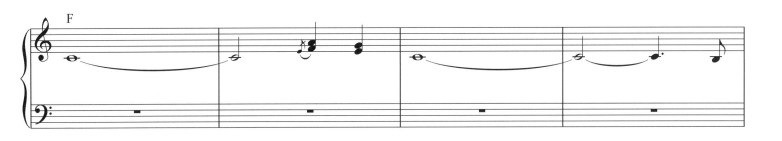

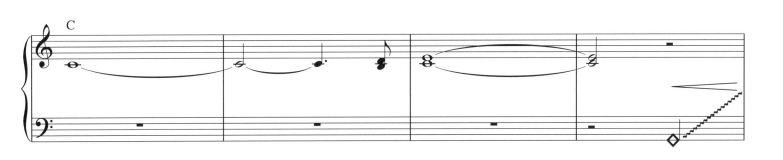

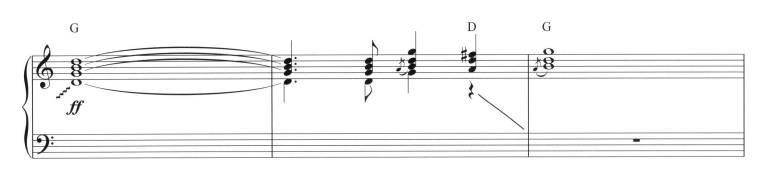

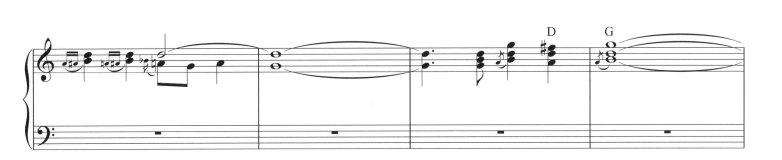

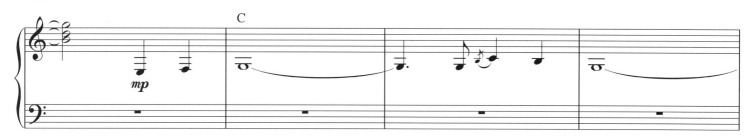

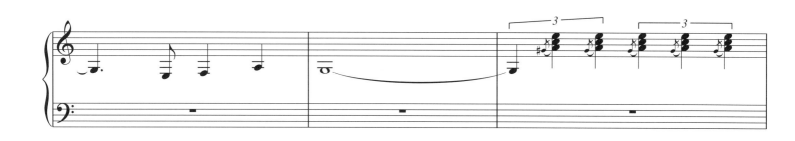

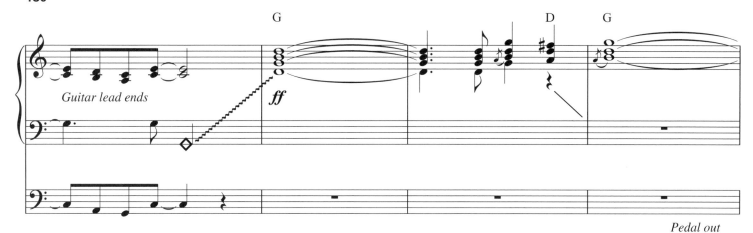

Guitar lead ends **ff**

Pedal out

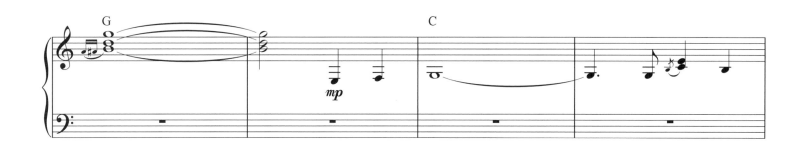

mp

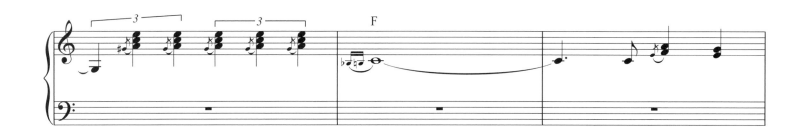

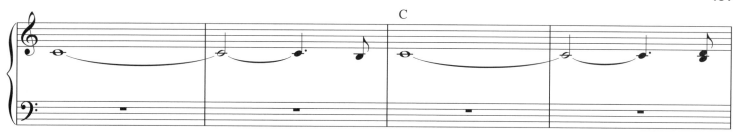

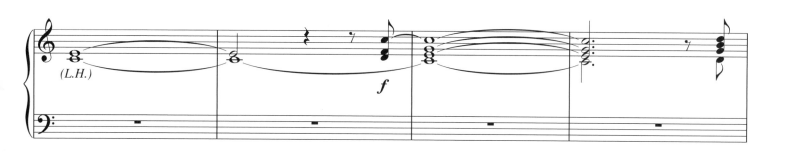

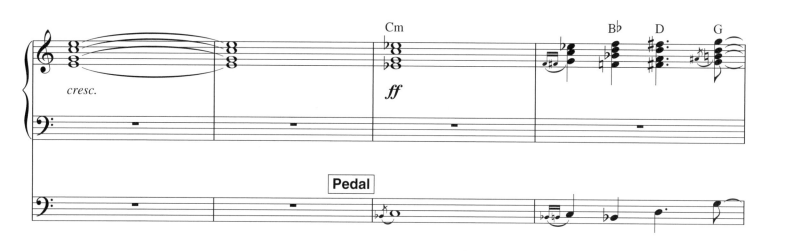

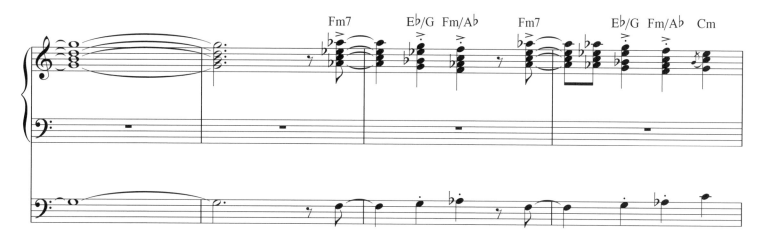

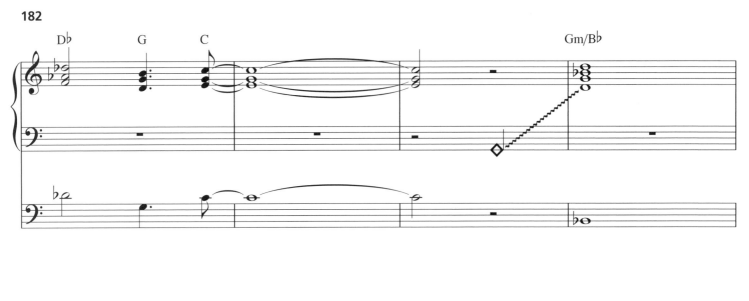

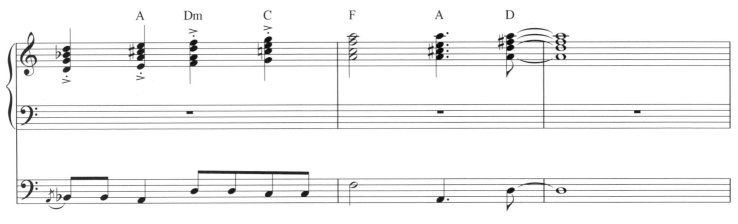

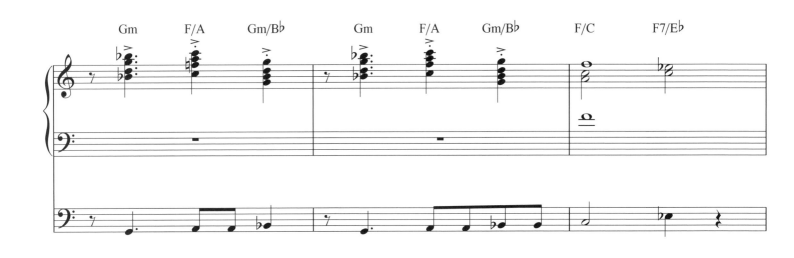

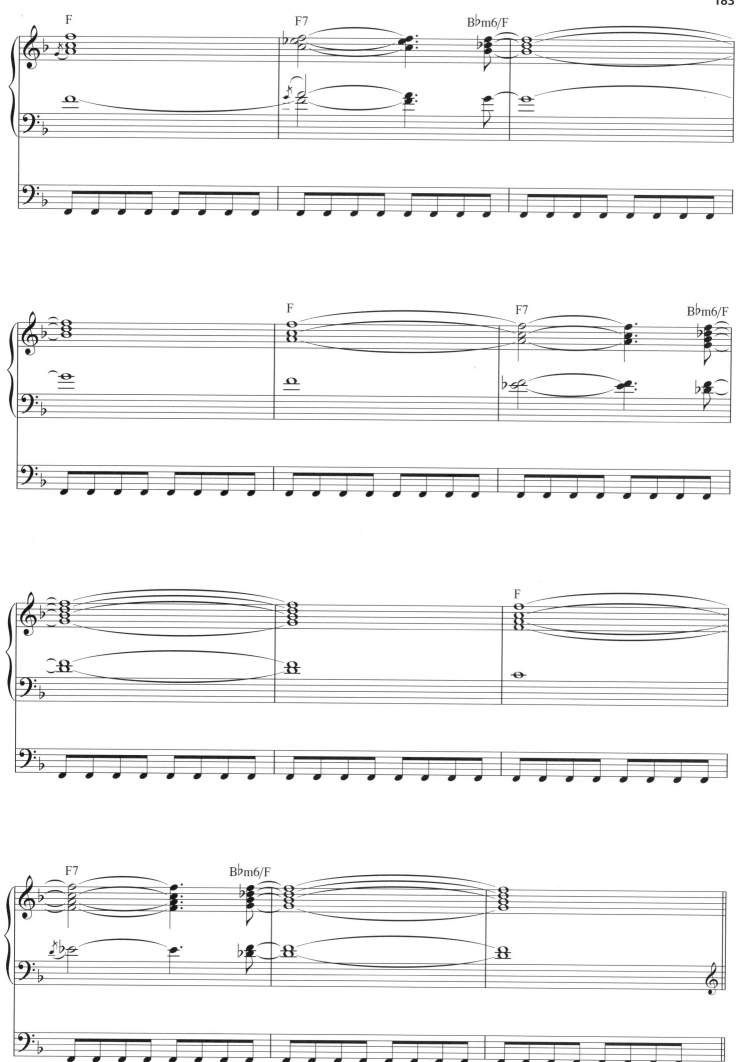

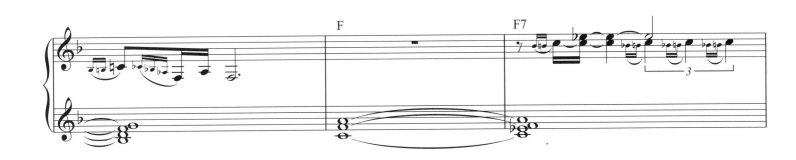

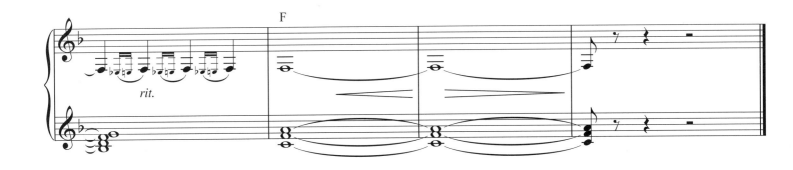

Topsy

Written by Edgar Battle and Eddie Durham

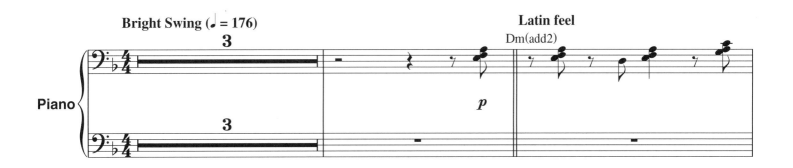

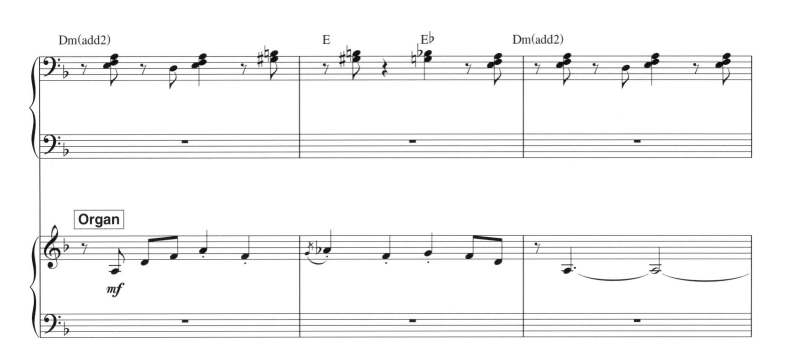

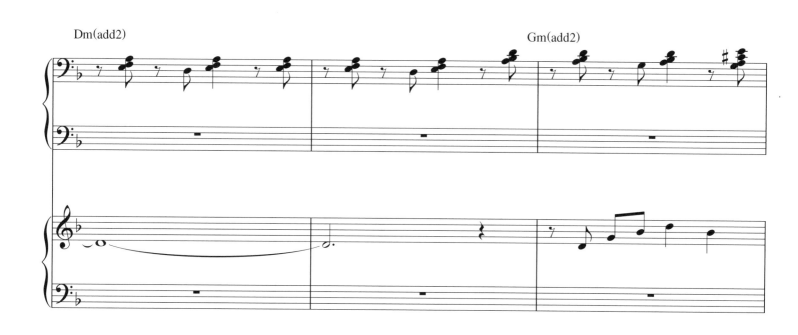

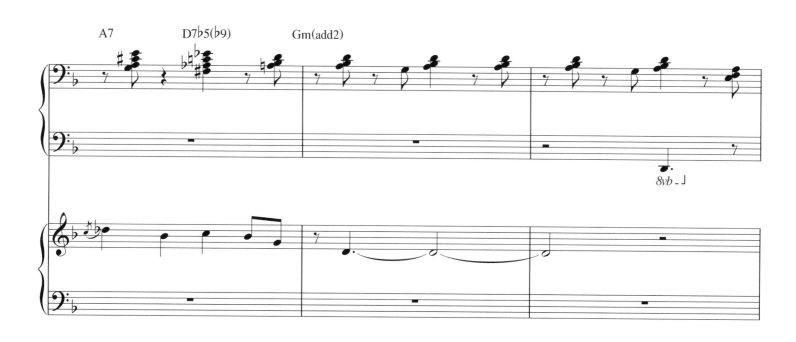

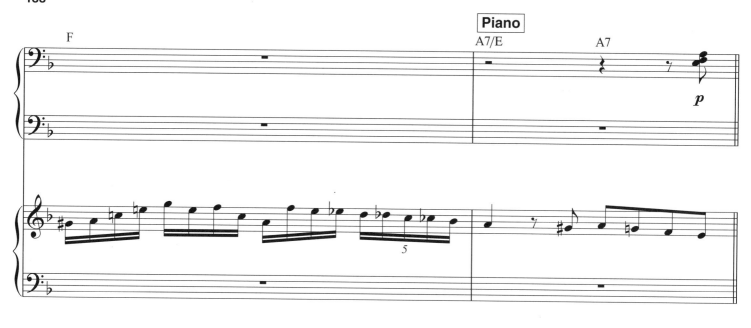

Big band arranged for piano

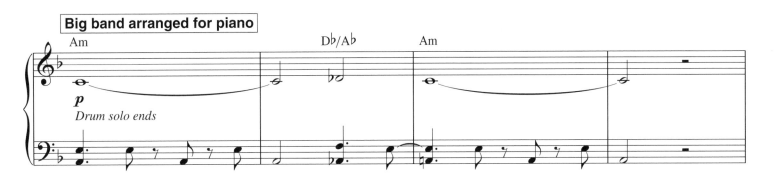

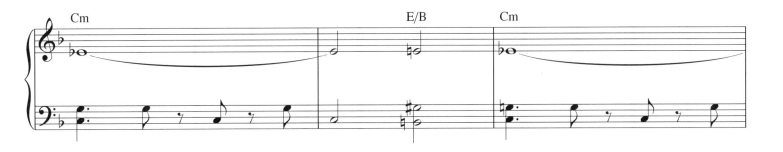

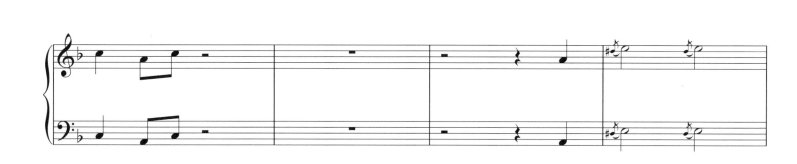

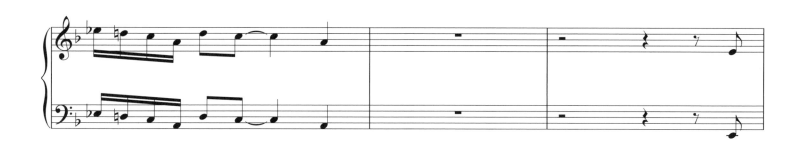

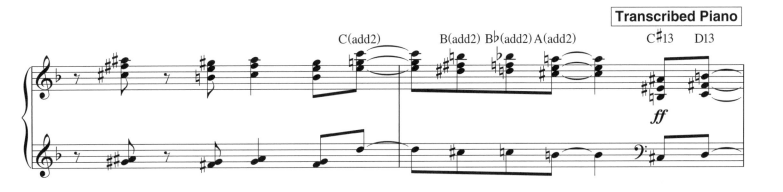

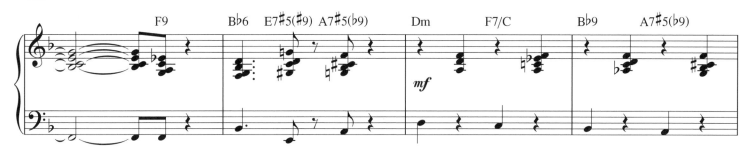

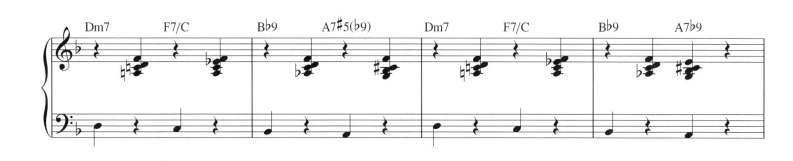

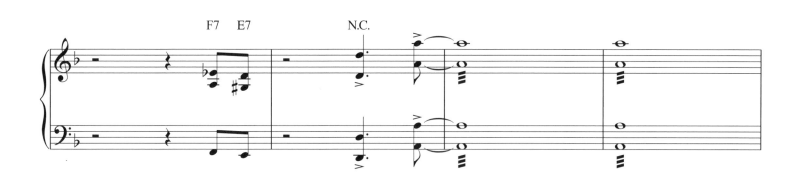

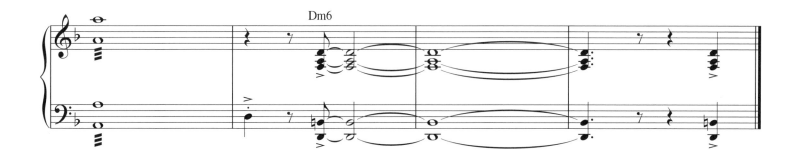

Tubular Bells
Theme from THE EXORCIST

By Mike Oldfield

Piano 2

mp

With pedal

Bass Guitar

mp

2nd time: begin fadeout

* *Original recording lists "Taped motor drive amplifier organ chord."*

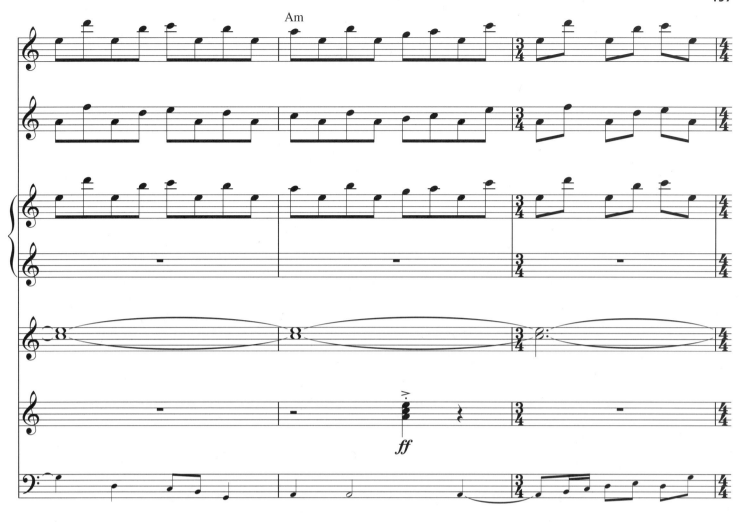

Honky-Tonk Piano 1 out

Honky-Tonk Piano 2 out

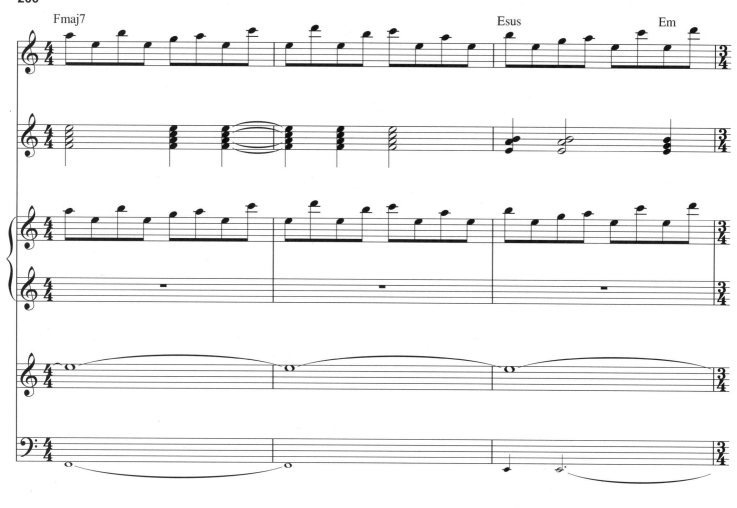

* Original recording layers "Speed guitar" (recorded at half speed, which plays back 8va) and flagolet (penny whistle).

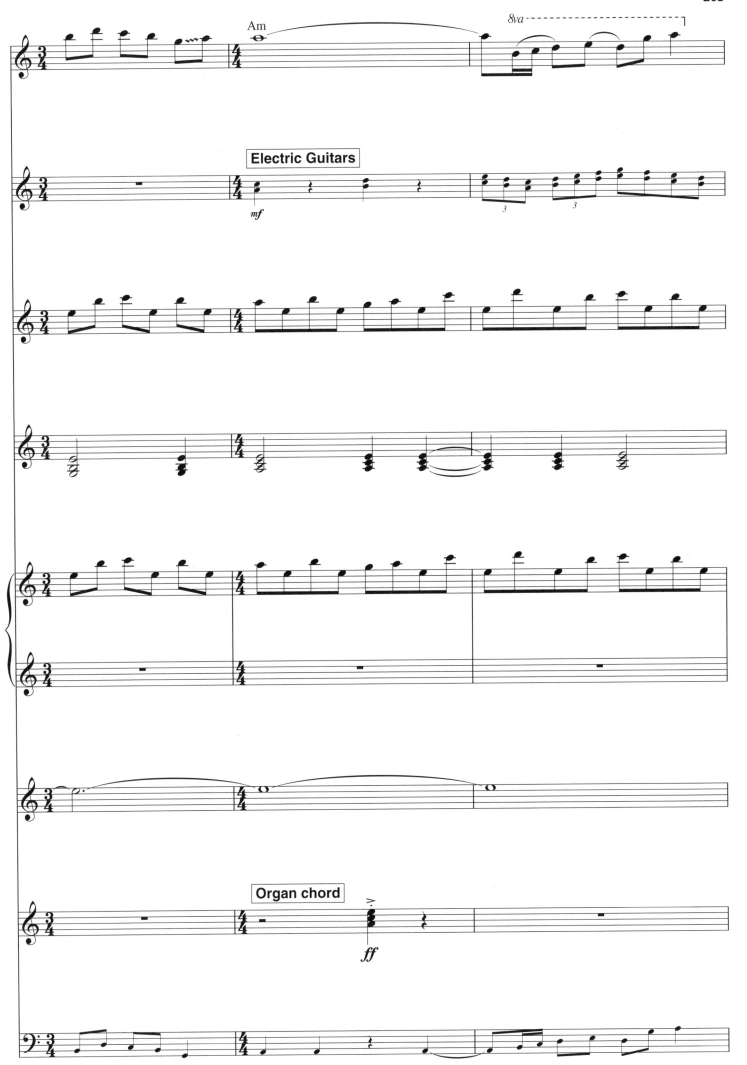

Bm(add2)/F#

N.C.

Lead out

Guitars and basses, arranged for Piano

cresc.

C#5

ff

D5

E5

3   *3*

D.S. al Fine (with fadeout)

Wack Wack

Words and Music by Donald Storball, Don Walker, Isaac Holt and Eldee Young

Wack! Wack!

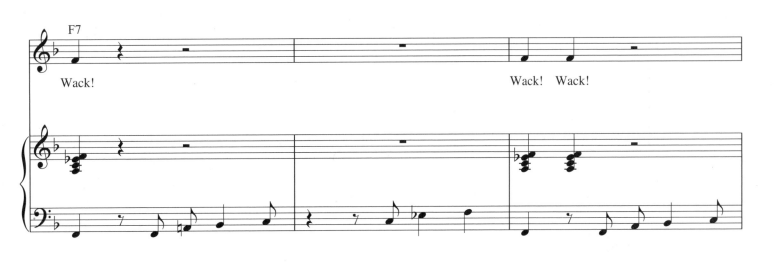

Wack!   Wack!   Wack! Wack!

Bass solo ad lib.

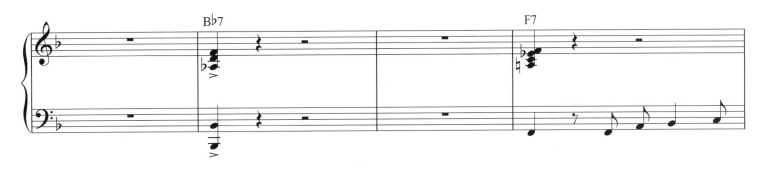

Piano solo ends

1. *Bass solo ad lib.*
2. *Drum solo ad lib.*

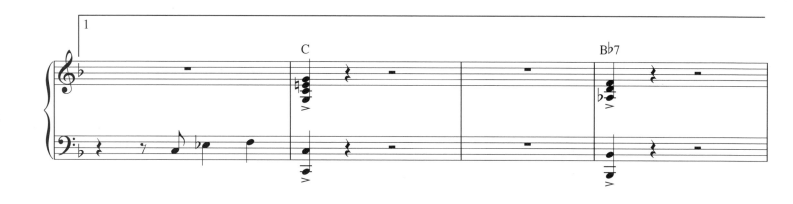

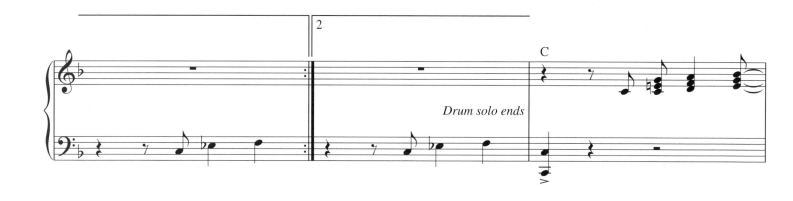

1. Drum solo ad lib.
2. Bass solo ad lib.

Solos end

Wack!   Wack!

A Walk in the Black Forest
(I Walk with You)

Words by Kal Mann
Music by Horst Jankowski

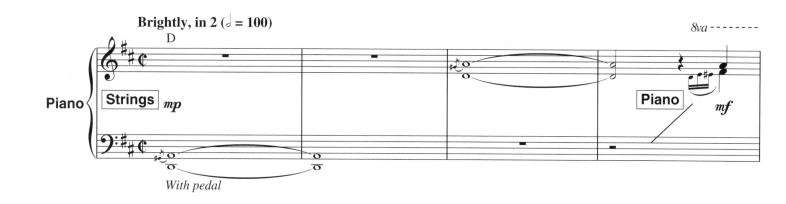

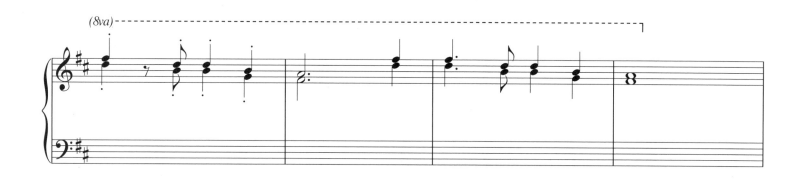

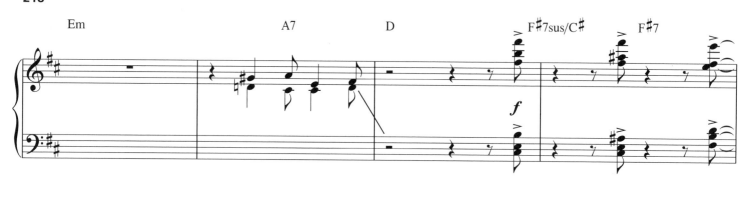

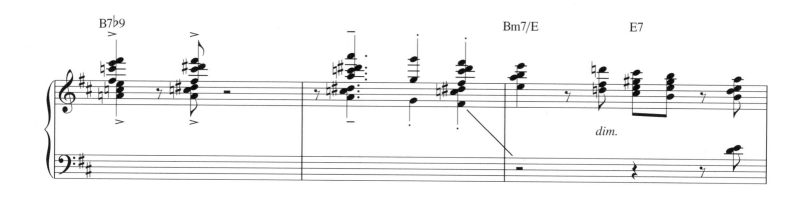

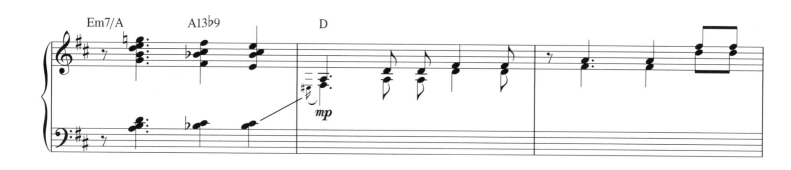

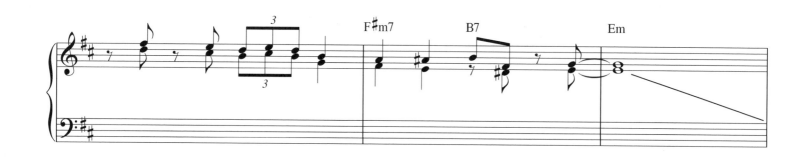

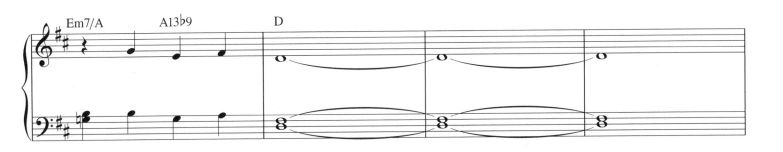

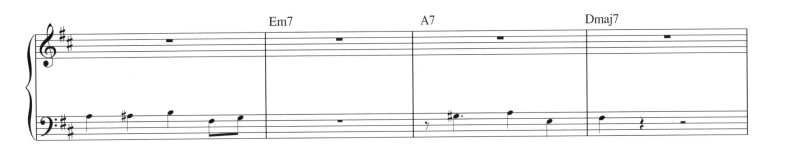

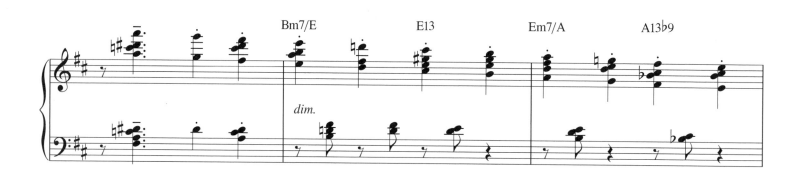

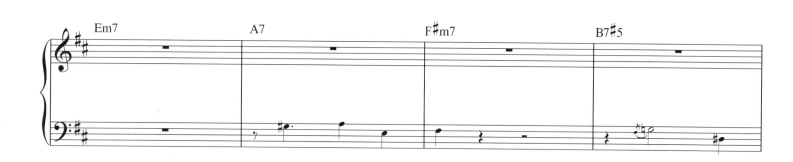

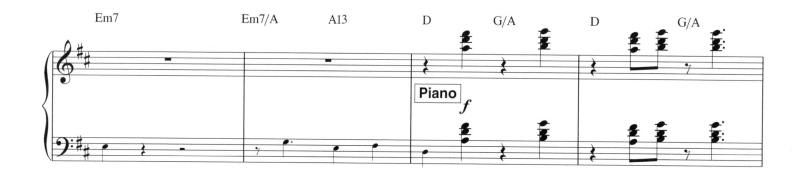

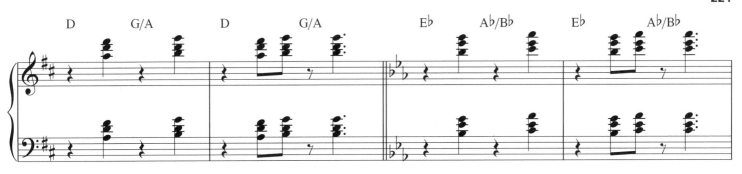

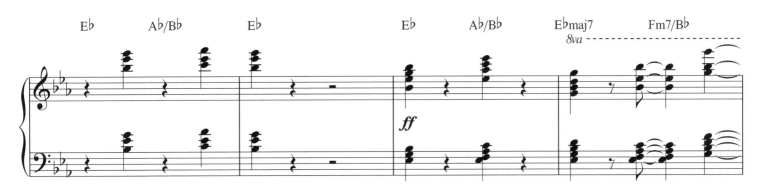

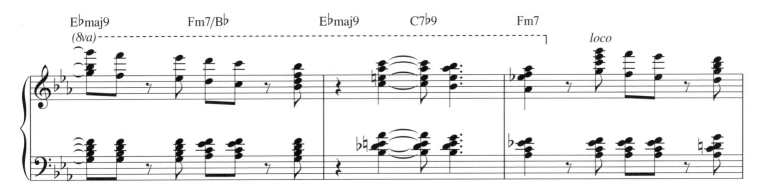

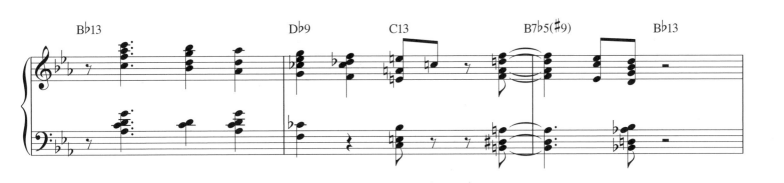

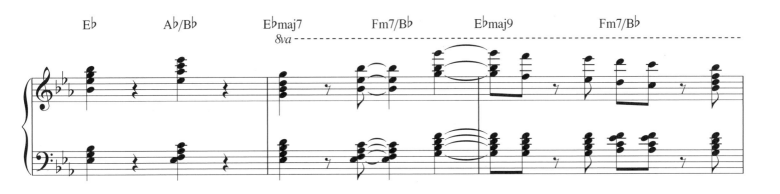

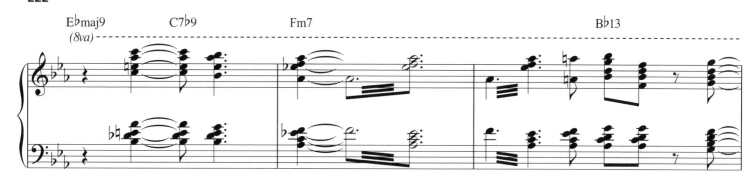

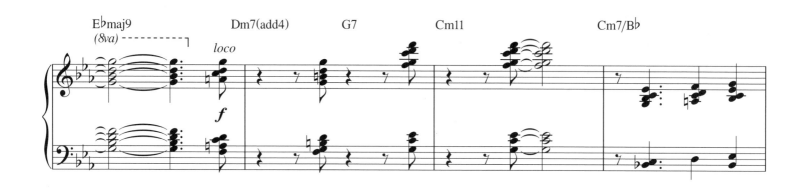

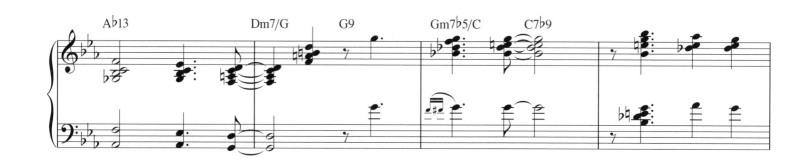

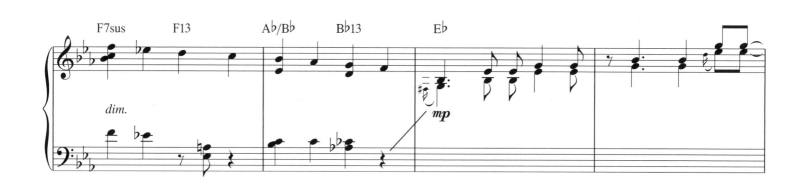

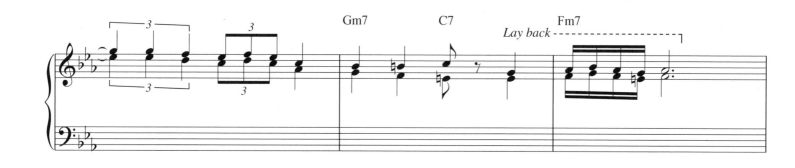

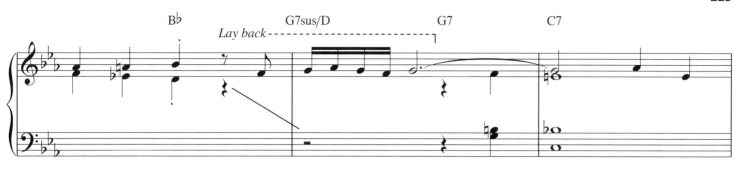

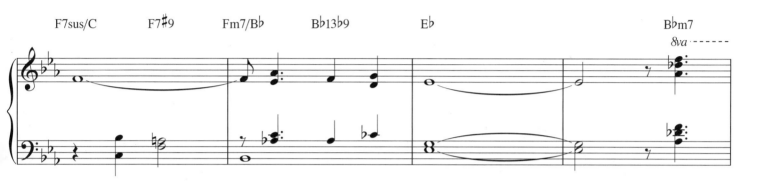

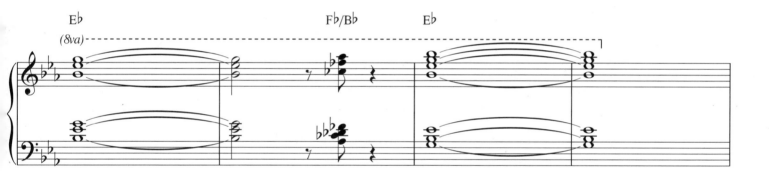

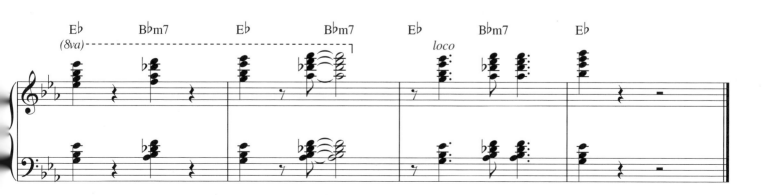

NOTE-FOR-NOTE KEYBOARD TRANSCRIPTIONS

These outstanding collections feature note-for-note transcriptions from the artists who made the songs famous. No matter what style you play, these books are perfect for performers or students who want to play just like their keyboard idols.

ACOUSTIC PIANO BALLADS

16 acoustic piano favorites: Angel • Candle in the Wind • Don't Let the Sun Go Down on Me • Endless Love • Imagine • It's Too Late • Let It Be • Mandy • Ribbon in the Sky • Sailing • She's Got a Way • So Far Away • Tapestry • You Never Give Me Your Money • You've Got a Friend • Your Song.
00690351...$19.95

THE BEATLES KEYBOARD BOOK

23 Beatles favorites, including: All You Need Is Love • Back in the U.S.S.R. • Come Together • Get Back • Good Day Sunshine • Hey Jude • Lady Madonna • Let It Be • Lucy in the Sky with Diamonds • Ob-La-Di, Ob-La-Da • Oh! Darling • Penny Lane • Revolution • We Can Work It Out • With a Little Help from My Friends • and more.
00694827...$22.95

CLASSIC ROCK

35 all-time rock classics: Beth • Bloody Well Right • Changes • Cold as Ice • Come Sail Away • Don't Do Me like That • Hard to Handle • Heaven • Killer Queen • King of Pain • Layla • Light My Fire • Oye Como Va • Piano Man • Takin' Care of Business • Werewolves of London • and more.
00310940...$24.95

JAZZ

24 favorites from Bill Evans, Thelonious Monk, Oscar Peterson, Bud Powell, Art Tatum and more. Includes: Ain't Misbehavin' • April in Paris • Autumn in New York • Body and Soul • Freddie Freeloader • Giant Steps • My Funny Valentine • Satin Doll • Song for My Father • Stella by Starlight • and more.
00310941...$22.95

JAZZ STANDARDS

23 classics by 23 jazz masters, including: Blue Skies • Come Rain or Come Shine • Honeysuckle Rose • I Remember You • A Night in Tunisia • Stormy Weather (Keeps Rainin' All the Time) • Where or When • and more.
00311731...$22.95

THE BILLY JOEL KEYBOARD BOOK

16 mega-hits from the Piano Man himself: Allentown • And So It Goes • Honesty • Just the Way You Are • Movin' Out • My Life • New York State of Mind • Piano Man • Pressure • She's Got a Way • Tell Her About It • and more.
00694828...$22.95

BILLY JOEL FAVORITES KEYBOARD BOOK

Here are 18 of the very best from Billy: Don't Ask Me Why • The Entertainer • 52nd Street • An Innocent Man • Lullabye (Goodnight, My Angel) • Only the Good Die Young • Say Goodbye to Hollywood • Vienna • and more.
00691060...$22.99

ELTON JOHN

20 of Elton John's best songs: Bennie and the Jets • Candle in the Wind • Crocodile Rock • Daniel • Don't Let the Sun Go Down on Me • Goodbye Yellow Brick Road • I Guess That's Why They Call It the Blues • Little Jeannie • Rocket Man • Your Song • and more.
00694829...$22.95

ELTON JOHN FAVORITES

Here are Elton's keyboard parts for 20 top songs: Can You Feel the Love Tonight • I'm Still Standing • Indian Sunset • Levon • Madman Across the Water • Pinball Wizard • Sad Songs (Say So Much) • Saturday Night's Alright (For Fighting) • and more.
00691059...$22.99

KEYBOARD INSTRUMENTALS

22 songs transcribed exactly as you remmember them, including: Alley Cat • Celestial Soda Pop • Green Onions • The Happy Organ • Last Date • Miami Vice • Outa-Space • Popcorn • Red River Rock • Tubular Bells • and more.
00109769...$19.99

ALICIA KEYS

Authentic piano and vocal transcriptions of 18 of her best-known songs, including: Fallin' • How Come You Don't Call Me • If I Ain't Got You • No One • Prelude to a Kiss • Wild Horses • A Woman's Worth • You Don't Know My Name • and more.
00307096 ....$21.95

FOR MORE INFORMATION,
SEE YOUR LOCAL MUSIC DEALER,
OR WRITE TO:

HAL•LEONARD®
CORPORATION
7777 W. BLUEMOUND RD. P.O. BOX 13819
MILWAUKEE, WISCONSIN 53213

THE CAROLE KING KEYBOARD BOOK

16 of King's greatest songs: Beautiful • Been to Canaa • Home Again • I Feel the Earth Move • It's Too Late • Jazzman • (You Make Me Feel) Like a Natural Woman • Nightingale • Smackwater Jack • So Far Away • Swee Seasons • Tapestry • Way Over Yonder • Where You Lead • Will You Love Me Tomorrow • You've Got a Friend.
00690554...$19.9

POP/ROCK

35 songs, including: Africa • Against All Odds • Axel F • Centerfold • Chariots of Fire • Cherish • Don't Let the Su Go Down on Me • Drops of Jupiter (Tell Me) • Faithfully • It's Too Late • Just the Way You Are • Let It Be • Mand • Sailing • Sweet Dreams Are Made of This • Walking i Memphis • and more.
00310939...$21.9

R&B

35 R&B classics: Baby Love • Boogie on Reggae Woma • Easy • Endless Love • Fallin' • Green Onions • Highe Ground • I'll Be There • Just Once • Money (That's What Want) • On the Wings of Love • Ribbon in the Sky • Th Masquerade • Three Times a Lady • and more.
00310942...$24.9

ROCK HITS

30 smash hits transcribed precisely as they were playe Includes: Baba O'Riley • Bennie and the Jets • Carry O Wayward Son • Dreamer • Eye in the Sky • I Feel th Earth Move • Jump • Layla • Movin' Out (Anthony's Son • Tempted • What a Fool Believes • You're My Best Frien • and more.
00311914 ....$24.9

STEVIE WONDER

14 of Stevie's most popular songs: Boogie on Reggae Womc • Hey Love • Higher Ground • I Wish • Isn't She Lovely Lately • Living for the City • Overjoyed • Ribbon in the Sk • Send One Your Love • Superstition • That Girl • You Are th Sunshine of My Life • You Haven't Done Nothin'.
00306698...$21.9

Visit Hal Leonard online at
www.halleonard.com

Prices, contents and availability subject to change without noti